KT-392-566

Cover illustrated by Valeria Petrone

Published by Ladybird Books Ltd
80 Strand London WC2R 0RL
A Penguin Company
9 10

Printed in Italy

Humpty Dumpty

and other nursery rhymes

illustrated by JAN SMITH

Oh, the grand old Duke of York,
He had ten thousand men,
He marched them up
to the top of the hill,
And he marched them down again.

And when they were up
they were up,
And when they were down
they were down,
And when they were only halfway up,
They were neither up nor down.

Humpty Dumpty sat on a wall,
Humpty Dumpty had a great fall,
All the King's horses,
And all the King's men,
Couldn't put Humpty together again.

Lavender's blue, dilly, dilly,
Lavender's green;
When I am King, dilly, dilly,
You shall be Queen.

Ring-a-ring o' roses,
A pocket full of posies,
A-tishoo! A-tishoo!
We all fall down.

The cows are in the meadow
Lying fast asleep,
A-tishoo! A-tishoo!
We all get up again.

Mary, Mary, quite contrary,
How does your garden grow?
With silver bells and cockle shells
And pretty maids all in a row.

Roses are red,
Violets are blue,
Sugar is sweet
And so are you.

Little Jack Horner
Sat in a corner,
Eating his Christmas pie;
He put in his thumb,
And pulled out a plum,
And said, "What a good boy am I!"

Simple Simon met a pieman
Going to the fair;
Said Simple Simon to the pieman,
"Let me taste your ware."

Said the pieman to Simple Simon,
"Show me first your penny."
Said Simple Simon to the pieman,
"Indeed, I have not any."

One, two,
Buckle my shoe;

Three, four,
Knock at the door;

Five, six,
Pick up sticks;

Seven, eight,
Lay them straight;

Nine, ten,
A big fat hen;

Eleven, twelve,
Dig and delve;

Thirteen, fourteen,
Maids a-courting;

Fifteen, sixteen,
Maids in the kitchen;

Seventeen, eighteen,
Maids in waiting;

Nineteen, twenty,
My plate's empty.

Bobby Shafto's gone to sea,
Silver buckles on his knee;
He'll come back and marry me,
Bonny Bobby Shafto!

Bobby Shafto's bright and fair,
Combing down his yellow hair;
He's my love for evermore,
Bonny Bobby Shafto!

Row, row, row your boat,
Gently down the stream;
Merrily, merrily, merrily, merrily,
Life is but a dream.

There was a crooked man,
and he walked a crooked mile,

He found a crooked sixpence
against a crooked stile;

He bought a crooked cat,
which caught a crooked mouse,

And they all lived together in
a little crooked house.

Barber, barber, shave a pig,
How many hairs will make a wig?
Four and twenty, that's enough;
Give the barber a pinch of snuff.

A-tish oooo!

Rub-a-dub-dub,
Three men in a tub,
And how do you think
   they got there?
The butcher, the baker,
The candlestick-maker,
They all jumped out of a
   rotten potato;
'Twas enough to make
   a man stare.

Cobbler, cobbler, mend my shoe;
Get it done by half-past two;
Stitch it up, and stitch it down,
Then I'll give you half a crown.

Yankee Doodle went to town,
Riding on a pony;
He stuck a feather in his cap
And called it macaroni.

One misty, moisty morning,
When cloudy was the weather,
There I met an old man
Clothed all in leather.

Clothed all in leather,
With cap under his chin.
How do you do,
And how do you do,
And how do you do again?

Little Miss Muffet
Sat on a tuffet,
Eating her curds and whey;
There came a big spider,
Who sat down beside her
And frightened Miss Muffet away.

Ding, dong, bell,
Pussy's in the well;
Who put her in?
Little Johnny Green;
Who pulled her out?
Little Tommy Stout.

What a naughty boy was that,
To try to drown poor pussy cat,
Who never did him any harm,
And killed the mice in his
    father's barn.

I love little pussy,
    her coat is so warm,
And if I don't hurt her
    she'll do me no harm;
So I'll not pull her tail,
    nor drive her away,
But pussy and I
    very gently will play.

Six little mice sat down to spin;
Pussy passed by and she peeped in.
"What are you doing, my little men?"
Weaving coats for gentlemen.

"Shall I come in and
    cut off your threads?"
No, no, Mistress Pussy,
    you'd bite off our heads.
"Oh, no, I won't,
    I'll help you spin."
That may be so,
    but you can't come in.

21

Good night, sleep tight,
Wake up bright in the morning light,
To do what's right with all your might.

I see the moon,
And the moon sees me;
God bless the moon,
And God bless me.

Star light, star bright,
First star I see tonight,
I wish I may, I wish I might,
Have the wish I wish tonight.

Twinkle, twinkle, little star,
How I wonder what you are!
Up above the world so high,
Like a diamond in the sky.

The man in the moon
looked out of the moon,
And this is what he said:
"Now that I'm getting up, it's time
All children went to bed."

Rock-a-bye, baby,
Thy cradle is green;
Father's a nobleman,
Mother's a queen;
And Betty's a lady,
And wears a gold ring;
And Johnny's a drummer,
And drums for the King.

"How many miles to Babylon?"
Three score miles and ten.
"Can I get there by candlelight?"
Yes, and back again.
If your heels are nimble and light,
You may get there by candlelight.

Notes on nursery rhymes

by Geraldine Taylor (Reading Consultant)

Collections of nursery rhymes are among the first books we share with babies and children. Each rhyme is an exciting story with song and action.

Nursery rhymes have a vital impact on early learning and they are a traditional part of childhood happiness for everyone.

Early skills

There's evidence that nursery rhymes help to develop the skills needed for reading, spelling and number. Rhyme and word-play help children to recognise sounds, and the rich vocabulary of the rhymes stimulates language development. Feeling and beating rhythm and hearing counting rhymes encourage early number ideas.